Marcu

GW01417937

Cicero

By United Library

https://campsite.bio/unitedlibrary

Table of Contents

Disclaimer

This biography book is a work of nonfiction based on the public life of a famous person. The author has used publicly available information to create this work. While the author has thoroughly researched the subject and attempted to depict it accurately, it is not meant to be an exhaustive study of the subject. The views expressed in this book are those of the author alone and do not necessarily reflect those of any organization associated with the subject. This book should not be taken as an endorsement, legal advice, or any other form of professional advice. This book was written for entertainment purposes only.

Introduction

Step into the vibrant world of ancient Rome and explore the remarkable life and legacy of Marcus Tullius Cicero, one of history's most influential figures. In this captivating biography, delve into the multifaceted career of Cicero, from his rise as a statesman and consul to his profound impact on the realms of oratory, philosophy, and literature.

Cicero, a brilliant and eloquent Roman, dedicated his life to the pursuit of knowledge and the defense of the principles he held dear. As a masterful orator, he mesmerized audiences with his persuasive speeches and became renowned as one of Rome's greatest speakers. His skillful use of rhetoric and his ability to sway public opinion played a crucial role in the political landscape of his time.

However, Cicero's ambitions extended far beyond the realm of politics. He embraced philosophy and became a student of various Hellenistic schools of thought. Through his writings, he introduced these philosophical concepts into the Latin language, creating a philosophical vocabulary that would endure for centuries. Cicero's treatises on rhetoric, philosophy, and politics not only shaped the intellectual discourse of his era but also left an indelible mark on subsequent generations of thinkers and writers.

In this book, you will witness Cicero's pivotal role in turbulent political times, such as the Catiline conspiracy and the struggles for power after Julius Caesar's demise. You will experience his unwavering commitment to republican ideals and his fierce opposition to those who sought to dismantle the traditional Roman government. Cicero's speeches and writings not only reveal his intellectual prowess but also his unwavering belief in the principles of justice, freedom, and the rule of law.

From his early education in Rome and Greece to his tragic end at the hands of his enemies, Cicero's life unfolds before your eyes, vividly portraying the tumultuous final days of the Roman Republic. Uncover the profound influence Cicero had on subsequent intellectual movements, including the Renaissance and the Enlightenment, as his works inspired generations of scholars, politicians, and philosophers.

This book is a meticulously researched and engaging account of an extraordinary figure who shaped the course of history. Immerse yourself in the world of ancient Rome and discover the enduring wisdom and legacy of Cicero, a man whose words and actions continue to resonate to this day.

Marcus Tullius Cicero

Marcus Tullius Cicero (January 3 106 BC - Formia, December 7 43 BC) was a Roman lawyer, politician, writer, orator and philosopher.

A member of a wealthy family of the equestrian order, he was one of the most outstanding figures of Roman antiquity. His vast literary output, from political orations to writings on philosophy and rhetoric, not only offered a valuable portrait of Roman society in the last troubled years of the republic, but also remained as an example for all authors of the first century B.C. (so much so that he could be considered the model of classical Latin literature).

A great admirer of Greek culture, through his work the Romans were also able to gain a better understanding of Greek philosophy. Among his greatest contributions to Latin culture was the creation of a Latin philosophical lexicon: in fact, Cicero undertook to find the corresponding Latin word for each specific term in Greek philosophical language. Among the fundamental works for understanding the Latin world, however, are the *Letters/Epistulae* (especially, those to his friend Titus Pomponius Atticus), which offer numerous reflections on each event, thus allowing us to understand what the real political lines of the Roman aristocracy were.

Cicero also occupied, for many years, a role of primary importance in the world of Roman politics: after saving the republic from the subversive attempt of Lucius Sergius Catiline (and thus gaining the appellation of pater pat*riae*, father of the fatherland), he held a role of the utmost importance within the *Optimates* faction. In fact, in the civil wars, he strenuously defended, until his death, a republic that had reached its last breath and was destined to turn into the Augustan *principatus.*

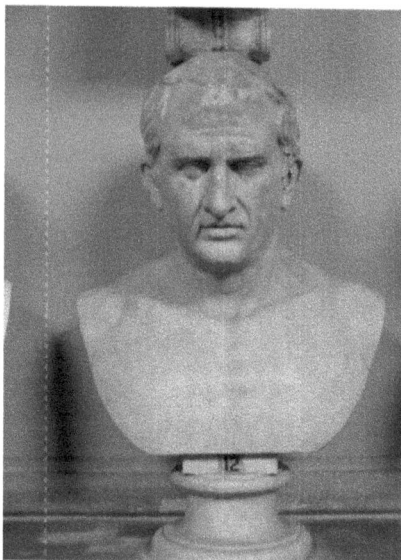

Biography

Childhood and the family

Marcus Tullius Cicero was born, on January 3, 106 B.C., in *Ponte Olmo*, near the Fibreno River next to the town of Arpinum (an area now occupied by the Abbey of San Domenico). The Arpinati received *civitas sine suffragio* in the 4th century B.C. and full citizenship rights in 188 B.C.; later, the city also obtained the *status* of *municipium.* Latin had been in use for a long time; however, in Arpino, the teaching of Greek was also widespread, which the Roman senatorial elite often preferred to Latin, recognizing its greater refinement and precision. The Romans' assimilation of the Italic communities close to Rome (which occurred between the 2nd and 1st centuries BC) enabled Cicero to become a writer, statesman, and orator.

Cicero belonged to the equestrian class (the local petty nobility) and, although distantly related to Gaius Marius (the chorifer of the *Populares* during the civil war against the *Optimates* of Lucius Cornelius Sulla), he had no connection with the Roman senatorial oligarchy; he was therefore a *homo novus. The* family consisted of his father Marcus Tullius Cicero the Elder, an educated man but of unknown origin; his mother Elvia, of noble lineage and integrity; and his brother Quintus.

The *cognomen Cicero* was the nickname of one of his ancestors who was quite well known for a fleshy growth on his nose (presumably, a wart) that resembled a chickpea (cicer, *ciceris* is the Latin word for chickpea). When Mark first applied, for the first time, for public office, some friends advised him against using his *cognomen* but he replied that "it would cause it to become better known than that of the Scauri and Catuli."

Studies

Cicero quickly revealed himself to be a child of extraordinary intelligence (so much so that he distinguished himself, in school, from his peers), which earned him fame and honor.

His father, wishing a brilliant career in law and politics for his sons, took them to Rome, where Markus was introduced into the circle of the best orators (and protectors of his family): Lucius Licinius Crassus and Marcus Antonius Orator; Crassus had particular influence on Cicero, who always considered him a model orator and statesman. In Rome, he was also able to train in jurisprudence, thanks to the school of Quintus Mucio Scevola. Among his companions, there were also Gaius Marius the Younger, Servius Sulpicius Rufus (destined to become a celebrated lawyer, as well as, one of the few whom Cicero considered superior to himself) and Titus Pomponius (who later took the *cognomen of* Atticus, after a long stay in Athens, and who became a close friend of Cicero's; in fact, he wrote to him in a letter, "You are to me like a second brother, an *alter ego* to whom I can say anything").

During this period, Cicero also approached poetry: in particular, he tried his hand at translating the works of Homer and the *Phenomena* of Aratus (works that later influenced Virgil's *Georgics*).

Particularly attracted to philosophy, to which he would make great contributions (among them, the creation of the first Latin-language philosophical vocabulary), in 91 B.C. he met, along with his friend Titus Pomponius, the Epicurean philosopher Phaedrus while visiting Rome; both were fascinated but only Pomponius remained, for his entire life, a follower of Epicurean doctrine. Between 79 and 77 BC, he met the rhetoric teacher Apollonius Molon (who also instructed, a few years later, Gaius Julius Caesar) and the academician Philo of Larissa, who exerted on him, a profound influence: in fact, he was head of the Academy of Athens that Plato had founded some three hundred years earlier; as a result, thanks to him, Cicero assimilated Platonic philosophy, so much so that he often came to define Plato as his own god (while rejecting his *theory of ideas*).

A short time later, Cicero met Diodotus, an exponent of Stoicism; this movement had previously been introduced in Rome, where it had received wide acclaim because of its emphasis on control of the emotions and willpower (in line with Roman ideals). Cicero did not fully adopt the austere Stoic philosophy but preferred a modified Stoicism; later, Diodotus became a protégé of Cicero, by whom he was housed until his death.

First experiences

Cicero's childhood dream was to "always be the best and excel over others," in line with Homeric ideals: in fact, he longed for *dignitas* and *auctoritas*, symbolized by the toga pretesta and the rod of the lictors; there was only one way to obtain them: to walk the steps of the *cursus honorum.* In 90 BCE, however, he was still too young to land any office in the *cursus honorum* but not to gain the preliminary experience in warfare that a political career required. Between 90 B.C. and 88 B.C., Cicero served under Gnaeus Pompey Strabo and Lucius Cornelius Sulla during the campaigns of the Social War although he felt no attraction to military life since he felt himself to be an intellectual (in fact, many years later, he wrote to his friend Atticus who was collecting marble statues for Cicero's villas, "Why are you sending me a statue of Mars? You know I am a pacifist!").

Cicero's entry into a forensic career occurred officially in 81 B.C. with his first public oration, the *Pro Quinctio*, for a case in which he had as an opponent the most famous orator of the time, Quintus Hortensius Ortalo. But his real debut in oratory of a political character (at least according to the written records that have come down), came with the *Pro Roscio Amerino*, which retains much of the scholastic in its exuberant style: in the oration, he successfully defended a son unjustly accused of patricide, showing great courage in taking up the defense (patricide was, in fact, considered among the worst crimes in Rome) while the real culprits were supported by Sulla's freedman, Lucius Cornelius Chrysogonus. Had Sulla wanted to, it would have been all too easy to eliminate Cicero, just on his first appearance in the courts.

Cicero divided his arguments into three parts: in the first, he defended Roscio and tried to prove that he had not committed the murder; in the second, he attacked those who had actually committed the crime (among them, even a relative of Roscio himself) and showed how the murder favored them more than Roscio; in the third, he directly attacked Chrysogonus, claiming that Roscio's father had been murdered in order to obtain his land at a convenient price once it was auctioned off. On the strength of these arguments, Roscio was acquitted.

To escape a probable revenge by Sulla, between 79 and 77 BC, Cicero traveled, accompanied by his brother Quintus, his cousin Lucius and probably also his friend Servius Sulpicius Rufus, to Greece and Asia Minor: particularly significant was his stay in Athens, where he met again with his friend Atticus, who, having fled from an Italy ravaged by wars, had taken refuge in Greece; Atticus later became an honorary citizen of Athens and was able to introduce Cicero to some of the most important Athenian personalities of the time. In Athens, moreover, Cicero visited what were the sacred places of philosophy, beginning with Plato's Academy (of which Antiochus of Ascalon was then head). Of the latter, Cicero admired the latter's facility of speech, without, however, sharing his philosophical ideas (quite different from those of Philo, of which he was a convinced admirer). After a brief stay in Rhodes, where he got to know the Stoic Posidonius, he returned to Greece (where he was initiated into the Eleusinian mysteries, which impressed him greatly) and where he was able to visit the Oracle of Delphi; on that occasion, he asked the Pythia in what way he could attain glory, and she replied that he should follow his instincts instead of the suggestions he received.

MARCUS TULLIUS CICERO.
Born Augt. 5. 7H. 51m. AM.
Anno Mundi 3843
From Cardan.

Entry into politics

Returning to Rome after Sulla's death, Cicero began his full-fledged political career in a basically favorable environment: in 76 B.C., after delivering the famous oration *Pro Roscio comoedo*, he presented himself as a candidate for the questura, the first magistracy of the *cursus honorum.* Quaestors, elected for a maximum of twenty members, were in charge of financial management or assisted propretors and proconsuls in governing the provinces. Elected to the office for the city of Lilybaeum (present-day Marsala) in western Sicily, he carried out his work with thoroughness and honesty (so much so that he earned the trust of the locals). While in Sicily, he visited the tomb of Archimedes in Syracuse: thanks to his interest in the man, some important information about the scientist has been unearthed (in particular, regarding his planetarium).

At the end of his term of office, the Sicilians entrusted him with the case against the proprector Verres, guilty of tyrannizing the island in the three years 73-71 BC. Cicero gathered evidence of guilt, delivered two preliminary orations (*Divinatio in Quintum Caecilium* and *Actio prima in Verrem*), and the ex-governor, attacked by overwhelming evidence, chose voluntary exile. The five orations prepared for the later stages of the trial (constituting the *Actio secunda*), were later published and constitute important evidence of the misrule that the senatorial oligarchy exercised following Sulla's reforms. In attacking Verres, Cicero attacked the arrogance of the corrupt nobility but not the senatorial institution itself (indeed, he appealed to the very dignity of that order to oust its unworthy members). He acquired, moreover, enormous prestige because defending Verres was Quintus Hortensius Ortalo, considered the greatest lawyer of the time: "defeated," Hortensius had to accept that his place was taken by Cicero (who, he earned the title "Prince of the Forum"); despite the episode, however, the two orators forged, later on, a good bond of friendship (in fact, it was to Ortalo whom he also praised in the *Brutus that* Cicero dedicated an entire unaccounted-for work, the *Hortensius*).

In Rome, oratory and forensic activity were one of the main means of propaganda for emerging politicians, as there were no written documents on political subjects (with the exception of the *Acta Diurna,* which, however, enjoyed little circulation). Against Cicero, however, remained the nobles' distrust of *homo novus*, heightened by the fact that the last *homo novus* to gain relevant political clout had been a fellow citizen of Cicero himself, Gaius Marius. However, even Sulla himself, a fierce opponent of Marius, had taken some measures that allowed and facilitated the entry of *equites* into political life, thus giving Cicero a chance to reach the heights of the *cursus honorum*.

The success achieved by those orations (which were later called *Verrines*), anticipating the principles of a humane government inspired by honesty and philanthropy, brought Cicero to the forefront of the political scene: in 69 B.C., he was elected to the office of aedile curule and, in 66 B.C., he also became praetor in a unanimous election. In the same year, he delivered his first political speech, *Pro lege Manilia de imperio Cn. Pompeii*, in favor of giving full powers to Pompey for the Mithridatic War; at that time, Pompey was supported by the horsemen, who were interested in the speedy resolution of the war in Asia, while the majority of the Senate was against him. The reason for Cicero's engagement in a cause hostile to the high aristocracy (which, moreover, was reluctant to welcome him into its ranks) probably lay in its importance to the publicans (holders of public contracts and tax collection) and businessmen, whose interests were threatened by Mithridates VI. The province of Asia Minor, threatened by the Pontus ruler, was, in fact, particularly active in terms of economy and trade.

Consulate

In 65 BC. Cicero presented his candidacy for consulship. In 64 he was elected consul for the following year (i.e. 63 BC). His position was illustrated by his brother Quintus in a work (of dubious attribution: did Cicero himself write it?), *Commentariolum petitionis*, written to advise him in his election campaign. By a play of the classes, Cicero turned out to be elected by the vote of all the centurias. Along with him turned out to be elected the patrician Gaius Antonius Ibrida, uncle of Mark Antony, future triumvirate and arch-enemy of the Arpinate, who was accused by Cicero himself (*In toga candida*, an oration - which has come down to us in fragmentary condition - delivered in the Senate as a candidate shortly before the elections of 64) of being a colluder of Lucius Sergius Catiline. The trust placed in Cicero by the equestrian class was repaid as early as the beginning of the consulship with the delivery of four orations (*De lege agraria*) against tribune Publius Servilius Rullus' proposed redistribution of land.

During his own consulship Cicero had to counter the attempted conspiracy set up by Catiline. The latter was an impoverished nobleman who, after fighting alongside Sulla and completing the cursus honorum, aspired to become consul. Catiline ran for consul three times and three times was stopped by dubious trials or possible electoral fraud and finally hatched a conspiracy to overthrow the republic. Catiline counted above all on the support of the plebs, to whom he promised radical reforms, and on the other lapsed nobles, to whom he held out the prospect of an advantageous overthrow of the established order, which would probably lead him to assume monarchical or near-monarchical power; moreover, it would seem that he was supported politically by Gaius Julius Caesar, who was, however, kept out by Cicero himself and had no consequences. Having learned of the danger facing the Republic thanks to the tip-off from Fulvia, mistress of the conspirator Quintus Curio, Cicero had the *Senate* promulgate a *senatus consultum ultimum de re publica defendenda*, that is, a measure by which special powers were granted, as was expected in particularly serious situations, to the consuls. Having then escaped an assassination attempt by conspirators, Cicero summoned the Senate to the temple of Jupiter Stator, where he delivered a violent indictment of Catiline, with the speech known as the Prima Catilinaria, which opens with the famous incipit

Catiline, seeing his plans unraveled, was forced to leave Rome and retreat to Etruria to his supporter Gaius Manlius, leaving the leadership of the conspiracy to some trusted men, Lentulus Sura and Cetego.

Thanks to the cooperation of a delegation of ambassadors sent to Rome by the Allobrogi Gauls, however, Cicero was also able to drag Lentulus and Cetheus before the Senate: the ambassadors, having met with the conspirators, who had given them written documents in which they promised great benefits if they supported Catiline, were fictitiously arrested and the documents fell into Cicero's hands. The latter brought Cetego, Lentulus, and the others before the Senate, but in deciding what punishment should be applied, a heated debate ensued: after many had advocated capital punishment, Gaius Julius Caesar proposed punishing the conspirators with confinement and confiscation of property. Caesar's speech caused a stir, and would probably have convinced the senators if Marcus Porcius Cato Uticense had not delivered an equally heated speech in favor of the death penalty. The conspirators were then executed, and Cicero announced their deaths to the people with the formula:

since it was considered a bad omen to utter the word "death" (and expressions of related meaning such as "are dead") in the forum. Catiline was later defeated, in January 62, in battle along with his army.

Cicero, who never ceased to boast of his decisive role in the salvation of the state (recall Cicero's famous line about his consulship: *Cedant arma togae*, transl: "let arms give way to the toga [of the magistrate]"), thanks to his role in suppressing the conspiracy, gained incredible prestige, which even earned him the appellation of *pater patriae. Nevertheless, his* decision to authorize the death sentence for the conspirators without granting them the *provocatio ad populum* (i.e., appeal to the people, who could decree the commutation of capital punishment into a prison sentence) would cost him dearly only a few years later.

During the civil war

Following the reemergence of contrasts between senators and populares, and the agreement between Caesar and Pompey to the detriment of the senatorial oligarchy, Cicero was sidelined. His last chance to re-enter the political game was offered to him in 60 B.C. by the three most powerful men of the day, namely Pompey, Caesar, and Crassus, at the conclusion of the agreement for the first triumvirate: they asked Cicero to support the agrarian law in favor of Pompey's veterans and the less affluent plebs. Cicero, however, refused not only lest he appear to be a traitor to the aristocracy, but also because of his attachment to the legal and social order of which the optimates proclaimed themselves defenders.

After this refusal and the constitution of the first triumvirate, Cicero kept himself out of politics, but this was not enough to save him from the vengeance of the *populares*: in early 58 B.C. the tribune of the plebs Clodius Pulcher, an enemy of Cicero's because of a previous trial for sacrilege, passed a law with retroactive force that condemned to exile anyone who sent a Roman citizen to his death without granting him the *provocatio ad populum. This was, in fact,* a very clever political move by Caesar (who precisely before leaving for Gaul waited until

Cicero had fled Rome) who, through his ally Clodius, thus eliminated from the political scene one of his most tenacious opponents, who might have opposed him during his rise to power. Cicero was thus tried for his conduct during the trial of the Catilinarians Lentulus and Cetego but, forced into exile, he did not rest, begging his acquaintances to favor his return. Clodius, however, also passed a series of other laws that stipulated that Cicero could not even go near the border of Italy, and that his property was confiscated. In fact, the villa on the Palatine Hill was even destroyed, and a similar fate befell those at Formia and Tusculum shortly thereafter. In 57 B.C. the situation in Rome improved, when the nobles and Pompey put a stop to the initiatives of Clodius Pulcher, allowing Cicero to return and restart his fight against the tribune of the plebs.

A sympathizer of the optimates also because of his personal friendship with Milo, one of the leaders of the faction held three orations in defense of three optimates. In 56 BC. Cicero delivered the oration *Pro Sestio* in which he broadened his previous political ideal: the alliance between knights and senators in his view was no longer sufficient to stabilize the political situation. What was needed, therefore, was a common front of all the landowners to oppose the subversion attempted by the *populares*: this proposal took the name consensus omnium bonorum. Also in the same year he delivered the oration Pro Caelio in which Cicero finds himself defending Marcus Celius Rufus from the charge of attempted poisoning of his mistress, Clodia sister of the tribune of the plebs Clodius Pulcher and Catullus' Lesbia. Although the woman was portrayed as the one who had first attempted to kill her lover as a political opponent of her brother the charges were flimsy and Cicero explained the act performed by Marcus Celius Rufus as a youthful mistake. In 55 BC he wrote In Pisonem, an oration against the governor of Macedonia Lucius Calpurnius Piso, Caesar's father-in-law. Patricians and plebs were clashing with the use of armed bands, and in one of these clashes, more specifically on the Appian Way, Milo, organizer of the bands of landowners, killed the tribune Clodius. At his trial for murder, held in 52 B.C., Cicero defended Milo by framing his oration on the difference between tyrannicide and murder; in this case it would have been tyrannicide and therefore justifiable. But, unable to deliver his speech with the proper force because of the clamor of the crowd and the fear instilled in him by the partisans of Clodius in the forum, Milon was condemned to exile in Marseilles (a version of the Pro Milone was not published until later, giving a way to verify how it was one of the most skillful and subtle orations on the legal level).

After being appointed augur in 53 B.C. in place of Crassus, he went to Cilicia in 51 B.C. as proconsul, just as relations between Caesar and Pompey were souring. During his stay away from Rome, the orator's thoughts turned to the threat of civil war. Back home, he did not cease to urge the parties to moderation and conciliation, but his invitations fell on deaf ears partly because of the fanaticism that drove Pompey to intransigence against Caesar's demands. When Caesar crossed the Rubicon, Cicero tried to curry favor with him, but then decided anyway to leave Italy to join Pompey. He landed, therefore, at Dyrrachium, but upon reaching the Pompeians, he realized how unfounded were the hopes he placed in them as saviors of the republic: each of them was there not in defense of ideals, but only to try to profit from the war. After Caesar's great victory at the Battle of Pharsalus in 48 B.C., Cicero decided to return to Rome, where he obtained a pardon from Caesar himself in 47 B.C.

Cicero revealed in his works and in letters to friends such as Cornelius Nepot about Caesar's personality:

Cicero's hopes of collaborating in Caesar's government were cut short by the absolutist and monarchical turn of power. The orator retired and began writing philosophical and oratorical works. Added to this was his divorce from his wife Terenzia and the death of his daughter Tullia, followed by the separation from his second wife Publilia, a young girl.

When Caesar was killed, on March 15, 44 B.C., as a result of the conspiracy hatched by Marcus Junius Brutus and Gaius Cassius Longinus, a new political phase began for Rome, and for Cicero himself, that would end only with the advent of the empire.

Opposition to Antony and death

Cicero was not, of course, taken by surprise by the assassination, by the *Liberatores*, of Julius Caesar: he was certainly aware of the conspiracy that was being woven, but he always decided to keep out of it, though he showed great admiration for the man who was destined to become the very symbol of the conspiracy, Brutus. And Brutus himself, in fact, with the dagger stained with Caesar's blood still in his hand, pointed to Cicero, calling him the man who would restore order to the republic.

He wrote Lucius Minucius Basilus, one of the Caesaricides, a letter congratulating him on Caesar's assassination:

The date of the missive is not known, but it is usually believed to be very close to or coinciding with the conspiracy. The expression "quid agas quidque agatur" would indicate it was written before Cicero went to the Capitol, where the conspirators had found refuge after the assassination, barricaded in the Capitoline temple and protected by Brutus' gladiators.

Cicero, in fact, also returned to being de facto a major representative of the *optimates* faction, while Mark Antony, Caesar's lieutenant and *magister equitum*, took the reins of the *populares* faction. Antony tried to get the senate to decide to organize an expedition against the *Liberatores* (who in the meantime had moved to the Balkan peninsula), but Cicero was the promoter of an agreement that, by ensuring recognition of all the measures Caesar had taken during his dictatorship, guaranteed impunity to Brutus and Cassius. Shortly thereafter, the two, along with the other conspirators, fled to the Hellenic peninsula.

Between Cicero and Antony, however, relations were not the best, and the two, on the other hand, were at opposite ends of the political spectrum: Cicero was the defender of the interests of the senatorial oligarchy, a staunch advocate of a republic monopolized by the wealthy, while Antony would have liked to make Caesar's plans his own and gradually assume monocratic power. Meanwhile, another figure was emerging from nowhere in the political landscape of Rome, the figure of the young Octavian (destined to become Augustus), Caesar's great-grandson and his designated heir in his will. Octavian decided to adopt a pro-Senatorial policy, showing no desire to imitate Caesar's moves.

Cicero, then, sided even more openly against Antony, defining Octavian as Caesar's true political heir, and as a man sent by the gods to restore order. Indeed, Cicero hoped for the establishment of a young *princeps in re publica* who, assisted by an experienced member of the senate, such as Cicero himself, would restore peace and reform the republic. He also began, between 44 B.C. and 43 B.C., to deliver against Antony a series of orations, known as the *Philippics* because they recalled those of the same name delivered by Demosthenes against Philip II of Macedon. Meanwhile, Antony, in his desire to wage a new war in Gaul to increase his own prestige, decided to march against Decimus Junius Brutus Albinus, governor of Cisalpine Gaul, and besieged him in the city of Modena. There, however, Antony was joined by the consular armies led by Aulus Hirtius, Gaius Vibius Pansa, and Octavian himself, who defeated him.

Back in Rome, Octavian found himself in the situation of having to choose between totally abandoning Caesarian policy, which would have kept the agonizing republic alive, and distancing himself from the Senate, to which he risked total subservience. He chose to continue at least part of the Caesarian policy, and formed, along with Antony and Marcus Aemilius Lepidus, the second triumvirate, a political arrangement under which the three men were to carry out a thorough reform of the republic. Cicero was forced to accept that it would now be impossible to implement his plan of a *princeps*, but that did not mean he withdrew his severe accusations against Antony in the *Philippics*. The latter then, despite Octavian's feeble opposition, decided to put Cicero on the proscription lists, decreeing, thus, his death sentence.

Cicero then left Rome and retired to his villa in Formia, which he had rebuilt after the episodes related to Clodius. At Formia, however, he was met by assassins sent by Antony, who, aided by a freedman named Philologus, were able to find him all too easily. Cicero, realizing the arrival of his assassins, did not attempt to defend himself, but resigned himself to his fate, and was beheaded. That locality took the name Vindicius (from the Latin "vindicta," revenge), a present-day hamlet of Formia. Once he was killed, on Antony's orders, his hands were also cut off (or perhaps only his right hand, used for writing and pointing during speeches), with which he had written the *Philippics*, which were displayed in the senate along with his head, hanging from the rostrums above the tribune from which the senators held their orations, as a warning to opponents of the triumvirate.

Once Antony was defeated, Octavian chose Markus, son of Cicero, as his colleague for the consulship, and it was Markus himself who inflicted punishments on Antony, having his statues torn down and decreeing that no member of the *gens Antonia* could ever again be called Markus.

Plutarch relates that when, some time later, awarded the title of Augustus, Octavian found a nephew reading the works of Cicero, he took the book from him, and read part of it. Once he had returned it to him, he said, "He was a wise man, my boy, a wise man, and he loved his country."

Personal life

Weddings

Cicero probably married Theresa at the age of 29, in 77
BC. The marriage - of convenience - was quite harmonious
for 30 years. Terenzia was from a patrician family and was
a wealthy heiress, both of which were particularly
important factors for the ambitious young man who was
Cicero. By Terenziae Cicero would have two children: the
first Marcus Tullius Cicero, who like his father would
become a politician in Rome, the second Tullia or "the
sweet Tulliola," as indeed she is described by Cicero in
one of his innumerable letters; she married first a Piso
Frugi and then in second marriage Publius Cornelius
Dolabella from whom she would divorce because her
father supported the Optimate faction while Dolabella
was Caesar's lieutenant, finally dying very young at the
age of 34. One of Terenzia's sisters or cousins had been
chosen as a Vestal virgin, which constituted a great honor.
Terenzia was a woman of strong character and took more
part in her husband's political career than she allowed
him to take in family affairs. She did not, however, share
Cicero's intellectual interests or his agnosticism. Cicero
complains to Terenziae in a letter written during his exile
in Greece that "...neither the gods whom you have
worshipped with such devotion nor the men whom I have

served have shown the slightest sign of gratitude toward us." Terenzia was a devout and probably rather materialistic woman.

In late 47 BC or early 46 BC. Cicero repudiated Terence. The reasons for the estrangement are unknown, but Cicero accused his wife of neglecting him during the war, of not even coming to greet him on his return, and of returning his house burdened with heavy debts.

Toward the end of 46 BC. Cicero married Publilia, a young and wealthy fatherless maiden who lived alone with her mother. According to Terenzia (who accused Publilia of being the cause of his divorce), the maiden's youth caused Cicero to fall in love with her, while according to Tirone, the orator's freedman, a desire to take advantage of the young woman's property was behind the decision; Cicero, moreover, had already been appointed Publilia's guardian and administered her wealth. Shortly after the marriage, Cicero's daughter Tullia died in childbirth. He was greatly affected, and in July 45 B.C., as friends brought him comfort, he decided to repudiate Publilia guilty of rejoicing in Tullia's death after only seven months of marriage.

His divorce from his historical consort Terenzia and his second marriage to Publilia, also destined to break up, made Cicero the object of fierce criticism, such as that directed at him by Antony in his replies to the Philippics.

Both of Cicero's wives died at a very late age, which was unusual for those times (Terenzia even centenarian; as for Publilia, she was still alive during Tiberius's empire, having married the consul Gaius Vibius Rufus in her second marriage, according to Cassius Dione).

Offspring

Cicero's love for his daughter Tullia is universally known, although his marriage to Terenzia, from whom she was born, had been a marriage of convenience. Tullia was the one person whom Cicero never criticized. He described her thus in a letter to his brother Quintus: "How affectionate she is, how modest, how clever!" When she suddenly fell ill in February 45 B.C. and died, after it had seemed that she might recover, giving birth to a son, Cicero wrote to Atticus, "I have lost the only thing that bound me to life."

Atticus invited Cicero to visit him in the first weeks after Tullia's death so that he could console him. In Atticus' large library, Cicero read everything the Greek philosophers had written about overcoming grief, "...but my grief defeats all consolation." Caesar and Brutus sent him letters of condolence, and so did his old friend and colleague, the lawyer Servius Sulpicius Rufus. The latter sent a letter that was later much appreciated, full of reflections on the fleetingness of all things.

After a while, Cicero decided to abandon all company and retire in solitude to his newly acquired villa at Astura. It was located in a lonely forest, but not far from Naples, and for many months he did nothing but walk through the woods, weeping. He wrote to Atticus, "I plunge there into the wild and dense woods early in the morning, and stay there until evening." Later he decided to write a book to teach himself how to overcome grief; this book, entitled *Consolatio*, was extremely highly regarded in antiquity (particularly by St. Augustine), but unfortunately it has been lost, and only a few fragments remain. Later Cicero also planned to have a small temple erected to the memory of Tullia, "his incomparable" daughter, but then did not complete the project, for unknown reasons.

Cicero hoped that his son Marcus would choose to become a philosopher like him, but it was an expectation without basis: Marcus, on his own, wished to pursue a military career, and in 49 B.C. he joined Pompey and his army and left with them for the Hellenic peninsula. When in 48 B.C., after the disastrous defeat of the Pompeians at Pharsalus, Marcus presented himself to Caesar, the latter pardoned him. Cicero, then, wasted no time, and sent him to Athens to train in the school of the peripatetic philosopher Cratippus, but Markus, far removed from his father's watchful eye, spent his time eating, drinking, and having fun, following the lessons of the rhetorician Gorgias.

After his father's assassination, Marcus joined the army of the *Liberatores*, led by Marcus Junius Brutus and Gaius Cassius Longinus, but after his defeat at the Battle of Philippi in 42 B.C., he was pardoned by Octavian. The latter, in fact, feeling guilty for allowing Cicero to be placed on the proscription lists of the second triumvirate, decided to favor the career of young Marcus. The latter became, therefore, augur, and was then appointed first consul in 30 B.C. along with Octavian himself, and then proconsul in Syria and the province of Asia.

Ciceronian humor

- Seeing a marble bust depicting his brother Quintus, a man of short stature, Cicero remarked, *"How strange! My brother is bigger when he is half than when he is whole."*

- The daughter's husband was also not tall, and seeing him wearing the armor and weapons of a legionnaire Cicero asked those present, *"Who tied my son-in-law to the sword?"*

- A certain Vibius Curion had a habit of lowering his age and Cicero, *"But then when we went to school together you were not yet born?"*

- Upon hearing that Fabia Dolabella claimed to be 30 years old, Cicero assented, *"It's true! I've heard her say that for twenty years."*

- Cicero was not of noble birth so the patrician Metellus Nepotus mocked him during court hearings, asking him who his father was. But Cicero: "As for you, *however, your mother has made it difficult for you to answer that question!*"

- To a dishonest opponent who attacked him in the Senate asking, "*Why do you bark so much?*", Cicero replied, "*Because I see a thief!*"

Cicero politician

As a politician, Cicero has always been the target of criticism from ancients and moderns alike. Accusations levelled against him range from inconsistency to vanity to short-sightedness. But his conduct objectively can be justified if one contextualizes it in the politics of the time, made in a mobile game of agreements and conflicts between power groups and noble families, who exploited party labels for personal aims.

"Cicero was attached to the republican government by tradition and memory, remembering the great things it had done and to which he, like many other people, owed his dignities, social rank, and name. So he could not think of resigning himself so easily to its fall, even though actual freedom no longer existed in Rome, and only a shadow of it remained. One should not blame those, like Cicero, who cling to it and make desperate efforts not to let it perish, for this shadow, this appearance consoles them of their lost freedom and infuses them with some hope of regaining it. This was what the Romans thought, who, like Cicero, after mature reflection, without enthusiasm, without passion, and without hope, went to join Pompey"; this is what Lucan has Cato say in those admirable verses that express the feelings of all those who, without hiding the sad condition of the Republic, stubbornly defended it to the end: "As a father, who has now lost his son, takes a kind of pleasure in directing the funeral rites, lights the stake with his own hands, leaves it only reluctantly and as late as possible, so, Rome, I will not abandon you before I have held you dead in my arms. I will follow to the end thy name alone, O freedom, even when thou art but a vain shadow."

Cicero's constant concern was the defense of the *status quo* and the rights of the large latifundial estates, eager above all to acquire from Roman notables the credit necessary to join the ruling class. He therefore worked for the preservation of the power and privileges enjoyed by the *optimates* class, according to a formula that, in essence, meant security and tranquility (*otium*) for all landowners, and implied that power (*dignitas*) remained in the hands of an oligarchy.
His purported desire that one should enter this elite by "merit" and not by birth, even when one does not want to merely understand it as an implied reference to his personal affairs, nevertheless remained a theoretical abstraction, a utopia, not least because of the absence, then as now, of any real change in the political and social fabric of the Republic.

Cicero was, moreover, an advocate of the political ideal of *concordia ordinum* (an understanding between the equestrian and senatorial classes that later became concordia *omnium bonorum*, or concord of all honest citizens), and he extolled it, in particular, in his fourth oration against Catiline: then, for the first time in late republican history, the senators, knights, and people agreed on the decisions to be made, decisions on which the salvation of the state depended. Cicero hoped that the *concord* could last forever, although he understood that it had come about, at that particular juncture, only because of emotional pressure: moreover, the *concord* did not rely on a particular political project, but only on sentimental and economic motives.

Philosophy before Cicero

Cicero was the first of the Roman authors to compose philosophical works in Latin: he was, in fact, very proud of this, but he apologized, at the same time, for devoting so much time to philosophy. Some, in fact, believed that it was disreputable for a Roman man to devote himself to philosophy, others thought that in any case one should not devote more than a certain amount of time to it. Still others, finally, were firm believers in the total superiority of Greek philosophy and considered precisely only *Greek* works worth reading.

Cicero was convinced, however, that if the Romans devoted themselves seriously to philosophy, they would then reach the same heights as the Greeks, whom they had already equaled in rhetoric. But the taste for philosophical speculation was totally alien to Roman society: the *vir* was, moreover, a man of action. The Romans knew philosophy through contact with the Greeks, but they considered it useless, if not downright deleterious, to live a life spent in constant pursuit of knowledge that brought no glory to the homeland nor any wealth. In fact, the Senate even went so far as to expel from the Urbe the Athenian philosophers who had visited there in 155 B.C., Charnead, Diogenes and Critolaus.

The same senatorial *nobilitas did* not want, then, the people and young people to take an interest in philosophy (which would produce in them a certain love of *otium*, distancing them from real life), but they were forced to admit that no man worthy of the name could remain a stranger to this science. The senators decided to call back to Rome the philosophers they had driven out to take real lessons in philosophy from them, forbidding, however, them to teach philosophy publicly. Even Marcus Porcius Cato, a proud opponent of the penetration of Greek-Hellenistic culture into Rome, studied Greek philosophy, as did all the members of the senatorial oligarchy of the time.

Enjoying instant success in Rome was Stoicism, but it was soon joined by the other doctrines, whose exponents arrived "en masse" in Rome during the first century BCE. In a short time, therefore, the situation had undergone a total reversal and there was no longer any man who was a stranger to philosophy.

Philosophical training of Cicero

Cicero did not behave any differently from his contemporaries, but, at least in his youth, he studied philosophy convinced that it was exclusively a valuable support for rhetoric: in fact, he began to compose philosophical works only late in life, when only composition, precisely, could be the employment of his spare time. In philosophy Cicero sought and was able to find the consolation he needed, the remedy administered to him by ancient wisdom.

As a young man, Cicero impulsively studied Epicureanism, a doctrine that had also had numerous disciples in Rome, including Amaphinius, Cacius and Lucretius. In the beginning, Cicero was, in fact, a pupil of Epicurean philosophers such as Phaedrus and Zeno. Later, under the influence of other teachers, he embraced, at least in part, Stoicism, but he was never a staunch supporter of it: like others in his time, he elaborated a personal fusion of the two philosophies, in an eclectic way. He showed, however, strong preferences for the scholarly doctrine taught to him by Philo: the theory of probabilism and verisimilitude were perfectly suited to a personality such as Cicero's, to whom the moral elevation of Stoicism was also perfectly suited. This particular mixture of several philosophies was Cicero's true philosophy.

M. TVLLIVS CICERO
Conful Romanus Pater Patriæ Parthorum
Victor, hominum difertiffimus.

Works

Philosophical writings

Cicero's philosophical works provide an important source on little directly documented Hellenistic philosophical theories. In particular, the *Academica* are an essential testimony on the skepticism of the middle academy. In many cases Cicero translates Greek philosophical terms into Latin for the first time. For example, the terms probable and probability, used with slight variants in all Western languages to denote philosophical and scientific concepts, derive their present meaning from Cicero's choice of Latin *probabilis* to translate the term πιθανὸς (*pithanòs*) in the sense in which it is used by Carneades.

Alphabetical overview of all philosophical works

- *Academica priora* (first draft of the books on the doctrine of knowledge of the Platonic academy).

  - *Catulus* (Dialogue), the first part of *Academica priora*, lost.

  - *Lucullus* (Dialogue), the second part of the *Academica priora*, preserved.

- *Academici libri* or *Academica posteriora* (late version of the treatise on the doctrine of knowledge of the Platonic academy, in four books).

- *Cato Maior de senectute* ("Cato the Censor, on seniority"). Cicero imagines Cato the Censor at the age of 84 and expresses his nostalgia for the good old days, when in Rome the eminent politician could maintain prestige and authority until later in life.

- *Consolatio*: a consolation to himself written upon the death of his beloved daughter Tullia, in which Cicero urges consideration of the transience of all things and the importance of philosophy. The work has been lost.

- *De Divinatione* ("On the Prophecies"): This work, probably the most original of all those composed by Cicero, highlights a very explicit opinion on the trust that must be placed in the aruspicine art. Although he also discusses Stoic views on the subject, it is noticeable that Cicero treats the topics with the familiarity of one who has been able to observe closely the workings of Roman religion (in the guise of an augur), and can draw from it a lucid judgment, which cannot but be negative. From this work and the third book of *De natura deorum* the early Christians drew arguments to combat polytheism.

- *De finibus bonorum et malorum* ("On the Boundaries of Good and Evil"). It is a dialogue in five books that poses the problem of what the highest good is, taking into consideration the two ancient philosophies Stoic and Epicurean, which classified it as virtue and pleasure, respectively.

- *De Fato* ("On Fate"), which has come down to us not in its entirety. The providentialist doctrine of the Stoics is argued.

- *De natura deorum* ("On the Essence of the Gods"): *De natura deorum* was written in 44 BC, just before Caesar's death, and sent to Brutus. Cicero orchestrates a conversation between an Epicurean, Velleius, a Stoic, Balbus, and an academic, Cotta, who expound and discuss the views of the old philosophers on gods and Providence. The disguised atheism of Epicurus is refuted by Cotta, who seems to represent Cicero himself. Cotta takes the floor, then, to refute Stoic thinking about Providence as well. If Cicero rejected with certainty the views of the Epicureans in this regard, we cannot, however, know with equal certainty what he thought about the religiosity of Stoicism: Cotta's words, which have come down to us, by the way, only in part, contain no reflections by Cicero himself. It has been speculated, however, that Cicero embraced academic probabilism at least in part, although his admirers were instead convinced that he had moved away from skepticism altogether. However, it is important to be able to note the extreme discretion of Cicero's attitude: he is persuaded that worship in the existence of the gods and in their action on the world must exert a profound influence on life, and that it is, therefore, of a fundamental importance for the government of a state. It must, therefore, be kept alive in the people. It is the politician and the augur who speak. Cicero does not find the arguments of the Stoics very convincing, and refutes them by means of Cotta. Finally, he says he is inclined to believe that gods exist and rule the world: he believes this, because it is a common opinion among all peoples. This universal" agreement" is equivalent for him to a law of nature (*consensus omnium populorum lex naturae putanda est*). As for the plurality of gods, although he does not express himself categorically on this point, it seems that he does not believe in it, or at least that, like the Stoics, he regards the gods as nothing more, so to speak, than emanations of the one God. He then conceives of this one God as a free spirit devoid of any mortal element, the origin of everything. He does not, however, spare the mythical tales of Greco-Roman polytheism; he mocks and condemns the legends common to all peoples. It was especially this part of the work, the third book, that fascinated 18th-century philosophers: it was not difficult to point out the ridiculous aspects of popular religion, and it can be said that even in Cicero's time this had become a philosophical commonplace. The some, rejecting with contempt these fables, which they judged coarse, also rejected all belief; the others adopted the Stoic doctrine. To Cicero, on the other hand, the existence of gods appeared as necessary: all people believed, and consequently he believed as well. In much the same way, Cicero next analyzes the subject of the immortality of the soul, borrowing many of the views expressed in this regard by Plato.

- *De officiis* ("On Duties"): *De officiis*, which - it seems - was written after Caesar's death in 44 BC, is the last philosophical work of Cicero, who dedicated it to his son Marcus, who was in Athens. The work, inspired by a work by the Stoic Panezius, is divided into three books: the first deals with what is honest, the second with what is useful, and the third draws a comparison between useful and honest. In the work, Cicero does not provide profound explanations with scientific rigor, but he enunciates a series of excellent precepts, which are indispensable for making a man a good Roman citizen, dutiful to his duties and thus able to live in the view of *virtus*.

- *Hortensius*: a kind of protreticus or exhortation to philosophy, modeled on a similar lost work by Aristotle. As evidenced by the proem to Book II of *De divinatione*, in it appeared Quintus Hortensius Hortensius, who devalued philosophical activity; Cicero spoke out against this thesis. The work was greatly appreciated in antiquity, especially by Augustine; it has been lost and the only fragments that have come down to us are from quotations from it made by Augustine.

- *Laelius seu de amicitia* ("Lelius" or "on friendship").

- *Paradoxa Stoicorum* (Theorems explaining the ethical paradoxes of the school of the Stoics): These are exercises in oratorical casuistry, often judged by critics to be of low standard.

- *Tusculanae disputationes* ("Conversations at Tusculum"): The *Tusculanae disputationes* were composed in 45 B.C., under Caesar's dictatorship, when Cato Uticense had already been forced to commit suicide and the republic had, after all, ceased to exist. The dictator had been lenient, but he had given the intellectuals to understand that he would not accept any "insubordination" on their part: to Cicero, who had written a book in memory of Cato, Caesar had responded with the Anticato ("Anticatone"), in which he criticized the illustrious dead man, showing what his attitude would be toward his opponents. For Cicero the situation was indeed complicated: his daughter Tullia had just died, and political life had lost all meaning. The orator therefore decided to retire to the villa at *Tusculum*, particularly beloved by Tullia, where he devoted himself to the study of philosophy. The topics of the *disputationes* thus reflected his state of mind: what is death? What is pain? Is there a way to alleviate the afflictions of the soul? What are the passions? How should the wise man confront these disturbing elements of his own imperturbability? Finally: what is virtue? Is it enough to make a life happy? Among the last reflections is one about suicide, understood as a means of evading death. Cicero deals with these issues in his usual eloquent style, but there is a strong sense of powerlessness in them: it is clear that his thoughts are always on Rome and politics despite everything.

- *De re publica* ("On the Republic"), modeled after Plato's *Republic: See* specific entry.

- *De legibus* ("On the Laws"): *De legibus* was probably composed in 52 BCE, after Cicero had been appointed augur. It is a writing that can be considered complementary to the *De re publica*, whose merits and flaws it traces: it is neither a purely philosophical work nor a simple treatise on jurisprudence, but rather a compromise between the two sciences. In the first book, inspired by Plato's work of the same name and by the treatise *On the Laws* of Chrysippus, Cicero demonstrates with a great elevation of thought and style the existence of a universal, eternal, immutable law, conforming to divine reason, which is confounded with it. It is precisely divine reason, in fact, that constitutes natural law, which existed before all systems of law. After this beginning, Cicero moves on to the analysis of laws in relation to the various forms of government, just as Montesquieu will do, much later. Having no other republic at his disposal than the Roman one, Cicero does not imagine laws other than the Roman ones: they are the perfect laws. Having finished his analysis, Cicero limits himself, in the second book, to enumerating the few that can be considered imperfect, especially among those governing worship. The careful analysis of the religious customs appears, in the light of the date of publication, to be a careful propaganda maneuver by which Cicero appears to his fellow citizens as a man well worthy of the priestly office entrusted to him. In the third book, some passages of which have been lost, Cicero analyzes the nature and organization of power, the character of the various functions of the state, and the healthy antagonism that must exist between the forces that constitute it. These questions, of such lively general interest because they touched directly on the problem of political freedom, were of considerable importance to Cicero's contemporaries. What was to be the part of the aristocracy or the senate, and what was to be the part of the people in the government of the republic? The time was not far off when Caesar would give the definitive answer to this question, and all those who foresaw what was to come attempted to strengthen the authority of the *nobilitas* and the senate. In the work, Cicero's brother, Quintus, is strongly opposed to the tribunate of the plebs, an office he sees as potentially too dangerous: Cicero, while departing from his brother's views, recognizes the danger that the tribunate of the plebs poses to the maintenance of calm and peace. We possess only the first three books of *De legibus: there* were probably six. The fourth was devoted to an examination of political law, the fifth to criminal law, and the sixth to civil law. These were particularly valuable works, because Cicero never dealt with the same topics elsewhere. Let us not forget that the treatises *De re publica* and *De legibus* were written at a time during which the Roman constitution was still standing, before the civil war and the end of ancient freedom. This circumstance explains the character of the two works: they are both theoretical and practical books, and also technical. After the advent of Caesar, the speculative element will dominate in Cicero's philosophy, who in fact will flee public life to retreat into contemplation.

Orations

Cicero is certainly the most celebrated orator of ancient Rome. In *Brutus* he considers the development of the Latin art of oratory to have been completed with himself (not without a certain self-celebratory purpose), and by Quintilianus Cicero's reputation as the classical model of the orator is already undisputed. Cicero self-published most of his speeches; fifty-eight orations (some partially lacunar) have been found in the original version while about one hundred are known from the title or from some fragments. The texts can be divided between orations delivered before the Senate (or the people) and between harangues delivered as-using modern terms-defense counsel or public prosecutor, although even the latter often have a strong political substratum as in the very famous case against *Gaius Verres* (the only time Cicero appears as an accuser in a criminal trial). His success is due to his argumentative and stylistic skill, which can be perfectly adapted to the subject of the oration and the audience, especially to his shrewd tactics, which are adapted from time to time to the particular audience, appropriately endorsing different philosophical or political schools in order to convince the opposing audience and achieve his own purpose.

Memorization techniques

To memorize his speeches Cicero used an associative technique that came to be called the *loci* technique or the rooms technique. He would break down the speech into key words and concept words that would allow him to speak about the desired topic and associate these words, in the desired order, with the rooms of a house or palace he knew well, in a creative and unusual way. During the oration he would imagine that he was walking through the rooms of that palace or house, and this would cause the concept words of his speech to come to his mind in the desired sequence. It is from this method of memorization that the Italian locutions "in the first place," "in the second place," and so on are derived.

Alphabetical overview of all orations

- *De domo sua ad pontifices* ("On his own house, to the pontifical college," 57 BC): harangue delivered for a particular purpose: during Cicero's exile, his opponent Clodius had consecrated part of Cicero's property on the Palatine to the goddess Libertas; Cicero declares this consecration invalid in order to obtain its restitution. It is from this context that the locution *Cicero pro domo sua is* born.

- *De haruspicum responsis* ("On the response of the haruspices," 56 BC): Clodius redacts a passage about the desecration of some relics during a survey of the haruspices on Cicero's land on the Palatine and calls for the demolition of a house Cicero was building there. Against this and other accusations Cicero makes an appeal to the Senate, in which he explains, that most of Clodius' accusations are based on wilfully deficient investigations.

- *De imperio Cn. Pompeii (De lege Manilia)* ("On the command of Gnaeus Pompeius (on the law Manilia)," 66 B.C.), political oration delivered before the people on the occasion of the attribution, made at the proposal of the tribune of the plebs Gaius Manilius, to Gnaeus Pompeius of special powers for the conduct of a military campaign against the king of Pontus Mithridates VI.

- *De lege agraria (Contra Rullum)* I-III ("On the Agrarian Law (Against Rullum)," 63 BC): oration delivered during the year of consulship, delivered in the Senate (I) and before the people (II/III); a quarter of the oration has been lost.

- *De provinciis consularibus* ("On the Consular Provinces," 56 BC), oration delivered in the Senate concerning the Roman consular provinces.

- *De Sullae bonis* ("On Sulla's Assets," 66 BC).

- *Divinatio in* Caecilium ("Debate against Caecilius," 70 B.C.), debate regarding taking on the role of accuser in the trial against Verres. Quintus Caecilius Nigro was under Verres quaestor in Sicily and presented his own candidacy in the role of accuser. For Cicero he was in fact entangled in the machinations of Verres.

- *In L. Calpurnium Pisonem* ("Against Lucius Calpurnius Piso," 55 B.C.), political indictment oration against Lucius Calpurnius Piso Caesoninus.

- *In Catilinam I-IV* ("Against Catiline I-IV" or "The Catilinariae," 63 B.C.), orations against Lucius Sergius Catiline: the speeches of Nov. 7 and 8, 63 B.C. delivered before the Senate (I) and the people (II); the speeches of the discovery and condemnation of Catiline's followers, Dec. 3 before the people (III) and Dec. 5 before the Senate (IV)

- *In P. Vatinium* ("Against Publius Vatinius," 56 B.C.), accusatory oration against P.Vatinius regarding questioning in the trial against P.Sestius.

- *In Verrem actio* prima ("First accusation against Verres," 70 BC), accusatory oration in the trial against Verres, accused of concussion (*crimen pecuniarum repetundarum*)

- *In Verrem actio secunda I-V* ("Second Indictment against Verres I-V," 70 B.C.), these five speeches were never delivered due to Verres' voluntary exile, but were nevertheless published in written form.

- *Oratio cum populo gratias egit* ("Thanksgiving to the people," 57 B.C.), thanks to all those who supported Cicero's return from exile and allowed him to re-enter political life.

- *Oratio cum senatui gratias egit* ("Thanksgiving to the Senate," 57 B.C.), thanks to all those in the Senate who supported Cicero's return from exile and allowed him to re-enter political life.

- *Philippicae orationes* I - XIV ("The Philippics," 44 B.C./43 B.C.), orations against Mark Antony.

- *Pro M. Aemilius Scaurus* ("In Defense of M. Aemilius Scaurus," 54 B.C.), oration delivered in the role of defender of Marcus Aemilius Scaurus.

- *Pro T. Annio Milone* ("In Defense of Titus Annio Milone," 52 B.C.), a defensive oration, originally different from the published version, did not have its effect as the curia was besieged by the loyalists of the Clodian faction. After Milo's exile it underwent profound changes to be published as it has come down to us: Cicero's finest oration. It contains among other things the famous quote "Inter arma enim silent leges"

- *Pro Archia* ("In Defense of Archia," 62 BC), oration delivered in the role of defender of the Antiochian poet Aulus Licinius Archia.

- *Pro Aulo* Caecina ("In Defense of Aulo Caecina," 69 B.C./ca. 71 B.C.), oration delivered for the plaintiff in a civil suit for a claim. The legal basis is the interdict *de vi armata* (possessor's remedy against violent dispossession). Supporter of the opposing side is Gaius Calpurnius Piso; both sides manifestly appeal to the authority of the jurist Gaius Aquilius Gallus.

- *Pro M. Caelius* ("In Defense of M. Caelius," 56 B.C.), oration delivered in the role of defender.

- *Pro A. Cluentio Habito* ("In Defense of Aulus Cluentius Habito," 66 B.C.), oration delivered in the role of defender.

- *Pro G. Cornelius* ("In Defense of Gaius Cornelius," 65 B.C.), oration delivered in the role of defender.

- *Pro L. Cornelius Balbo* ("In Defense of Lucius Cornelius Balbo," 56 B.C.), oration delivered in the role of defender.

- *Pro P. Cornelius Sulla* ("In Defense of Publius Cornelius Sulla," 62 B.C.), oration delivered in the role of defender.

- *Pro Marcus Fonteius* ("In Defense of Marcus Fonteius," 69 BC), oration delivered in the role of defender.

- *Pro Q. Ligarius* ("In Defense of Quintus Ligarius" 46 B.C.), oration delivered in the role of defender of Quintus Ligarius, addressed to Caesar as dictator.

- *Pro Marcus Marcellus* ("In Defense of Marcus Marcellus," 46 BC), oration delivered in the role of Marcus Marcellus' defender, addressed to Caesar as dictator.

- *Pro muliere Arretina* ("In defense of a woman from Arezzo," 80 BC), oration delivered in the role of defender.

- *Pro Lucio Murena* ("In favor of Murena," 63 BC), oration delivered in the role of defense counsel in an election bribery trial.

- *Pro Gnaeus Plancio* ("In Defense of Gnaeus Plancio," 54 BC), oration delivered in the role of defender.

- *Pro Publio Quinctio* ("In Defense of Publius Quintius," 81 B.C.), Cicero's earliest traditional legal discourse on behalf of the plaintiff in a civil trial. At issue is the legality of the preventive seizure action executed by the defendant Sextus Nevius against Cicero's client Publius Quintus. Defending the opposing party is Quintus

Hortensius Ortalo, and the judge is Gaius Aquilius Gallus.

- *Pro C. Rabirio perduellionis reo* ("In defense of Gaius Rabirio, guilty of high treason," 63 B.C.), oration delivered in the role of defender.

- *Pro Rabirio Postumo* ("In Defense of Rabirio Postumo"), 54 B.C./53 B.C. or 53 B.C./52 B.C.), defensive oration delivered at the preliminary stage of the trial against Aulus Gabinius on the grounds of concussion in the provinces. It revolves around the presence of "bribes" in connection with the reinstatement of Ptolemy XII Auletes to the throne of Egypt.

- *Pro rege Deiotaro* ("In Defense of King Deiotaro," 45 B.C.), oration in defense of King Deiotaro, addressed to Caesar

- *Pro Sex. Roscio Amerino* ("In Defense of Sextus Roscio of Amelia," 80 B.C.), defense oration, is Cicero's first argument in a murder trial. Sextus Roscius was accused of patricide. During the civil war, a relative had taken possession of the estate of Roscio's father and was now trying to secure the ill-gotten gains, which belonged to the legitimate heirs of the deceased. Cicero obtained an acquittal.

- *Pro Q. Roscio Comoedo* ("In Defense of the Actor Quintus Roscio," ca. 77 B.C. or 76 B.C.), an oration delivered in the role of defender.

- *Pro P. Sestius* ("In Defense of Publius Sestius," 56 B.C.), oration delivered in the role of defender.

- *Pro Titinia* ("In Defense of Titinia," 79 BC), oration delivered in the role of defender.

- *Pro Marcus Tullius* ("In Defense of Marcus Tullius," 72 B.C./71 B.C.), oration delivered in the role of defender.

- *Pro L. Valerius Flaccus* ("In Defense of Lucius Valerius Flaccus," 59 B.C.), oration delivered in the role of defender.

Writings on rhetoric

Just as it is difficult for Cicero to distinguish between life and works, so in particular differentiating between philosophical and rhetorical writings is yes practical and clear, yet it does not fully represent Cicero's conception and opinion. Already in his earliest preserved work (*De inventione* I 1-5) he makes it clear that wisdom, eloquence, and the art of governing have developed a natural bond, which undoubtedly contributed to the development of men's culture and which must be restored. He has this unity in mind as an ideal model both in his theoretical writings and also in his own *activa life in the* service of the Republic-or at least that is how he wanted to idealize and see his own reality.

Therefore, it is not at all surprising if Cicero developed his philosophical writings by the means of rhetoric and structured his theories of rhetoric on philosophical principles. The separation between wisdom and eloquence Cicero blames it on the "rupture between language and intellect" made by Socratic philosophy (*De oratore* III 61) and attempts through his writings to "heal" this rupture; and thus for better implementation philosophy and rhetoric according to him must be dependent on each other (see e.g. *De oratore* III 54-143); Cicero himself declares that "I became an orator [...] not in the schools of rhetoricians but in the halls of the Academy": by this he alludes to his training on the doctrines of the New Academy of Carnead and Philo of Larissa, his teacher.

Alphabetical overview of works on rhetoric that have come down to us

- *Brutus*: the book dedicated to Marcus Junius Brutus was written in early 46 BCE and deals, in the form of a dialogue between Cicero, Brutus and Atticus, with the history of the Roman art of rhetoric up to Cicero himself. After an introduction (1-9) Cicero begins a comparison with Greek rhetoric (25-31) and points out that the art of oratory since it is the most complex of all the arts only late came to perfection. While he considers the ancient Roman orators barely mediocre, he speaks of Cato as the basis of his own experience. Lucius Licinius Crassus and Marcus Antonius Orator, both protagonists of *De oratore*, are compared in detail (139ff.). After an excursion on the importance of audience judgment (183-200) and a reflection on the orator Hortensius (201-283), Cicero firmly rejects the model of Atticism (284-300). The work culminates in a comparison of the oratorical art of Hortensius and Cicero himself, not without a considerable dose of self-celebration (301-328); in fact, he presents himself as the culmination of a process of development of the oratorical art. The main point of the work is the criticism of the spread in the Neo-Attic style, to which the young Brutus also belongs, defending his much richer and more magniloquent style from the criticism of being an example of the Aesian style.

- *De inventione:* ("The Rhetorical Invention"): developed between 85 B.C. and 80 B.C. this is the first of two books of a comprehensive description of rhetoric, which was never completed. Cicero gave up completing it in order to devote himself to a more engaging portrayal in *De oratore*, and yet the work served, despite its fragmentary nature, as a teaching text until the Middle Ages. The completed section deals in the first book with the main concepts of rhetoric (I 5-9), the doctrine of teaching rhetoric with reference to Hermagoras of Temnus (I 10-19) as well as the role of the orator (I 19-109); the second book deals with the techniques of argumentation, especially in legal harangues (II 11-154) as well as briefly with orations before the people (II 157-176) and at celebrations (II 177-178). Cicero's statements regarding the content of the work bear many similarities to the Rhetorica ad Herennium, but for a long time erroneously believed to be his, which has led to numerous discussions among scholars regarding the relationship between the two works. Both writings are from roughly the same period and are based directly or indirectly on the same or related Greek sources. In addition, there is a remarkable literal similarity in some periods, which also probably suggests a common Latin source, perhaps originating from a common doctrinal teaching that mediated the preponderant content of Greek origin.

- *De optimo genere oratorum* ("On the best art of oratory"): this short work, probably written in 46 B.C. or, according to other opinions, as early as 50 B.C., is an introduction to the translation of the orations of Demosthenes and Aeschines, for and against Ctesiphon. The introduction is mainly about the Roman Atticists, with roughly the same arguments as the *Orator*. The translation, however, has not come down to us, and it is unclear whether Cicero ever actually completed it. The authenticity of the work has been questioned several times, but today it is mostly accepted.

- *De oratore* (On the Orator): the most important work on rhetoric by Cicero should not be confused with the almost eponymous work *Orator*. *It is a* work composed in 55 B.C. in dialogue form, as was the case with *Brutus*. The protagonists this time are Lucius Licinius Crassus and Mark Antony, examples, according to Cicero, of the greatest orators of the previous generation. In Book I, it is Crassus (Cicero's spokesman) who expounds the main thesis of the work, namely, that the good orator must have a thorough knowledge of the subject he or she wants to deal with, opposing the conception of some Greek rhetoricians who believed that training based on rules, technicalities and exercises was sufficient to deal with any speech. Book II, on the other hand, deals with the "parts" into which rhetoric is divided, namely *inventio*, *dispositio*, and *memoria*; Book III discusses style, that is, *elocutio*, and *actio*, that is, the way in which the orator should behave during oration. The *de oratore* is considered Cicero's most carefully written formal work, and for this reason it has always been used and studied as the primary model of Ciceronian style.

- *Orator* ("The Orator"): It was written in the summer of 46 B.C. and is also dedicated to Marcus Junius Brutus and describes an ideal model of the perfect orator, taking up many of the themes already covered in *De oratore*. Contrary to the dispute of that time between the Atticists, who - like Brutus - demand from the orator a sober and precise style, and the Asians, who prefer a very refined and magniloquent style, Cicero believes that the perfect orator, like Demosthenes, must master all styles and be able to switch from one to the other naturally. For this reason, one must devote oneself above all to philosophical training: only in this way will they be able to perform the three tasks of the orator: *probare, delectare, flectere* (demonstrate, amuse, convince), which are well ordered and described (76-99). Cicero also speaks briefly here of *inventio* (44-49), *dispositio* (50) but deals mainly with *elocutio* (51-236), dwelling on rhetorical figures and the rhythmic construction of the period.

- *Partitiones oratoriae* ("Partition of the art of oratory"): This work was written in 54 B.C., when Cicero's son Markus was studying rhetoric, and is designed as a kind of 'catechism,' dealing with the theory of rhetoric, mainly with schematic divisions in the form of question and answer between father and son. Cicero's originality in this work stands out much less, because of the very simple style and the few innovations introduced.

- The *Topica* (44 B.C.): written during the course of a trip to Greece at the urging of his friend Trebatius, they deal with the doctrine of *inventio* popularized by Aristotle, or the art of knowing how to find arguments. In this rhetorical production, places (*topoi*) are considered as excellent cues for all kinds of arguments and usable for any discipline (poetry, politics, rhetoric, philosophy, etc.).

Lost works

Cicero's late works include consolatory writings, contributions to historiography, poems (some even about his consulate period) and translations. These works are mostly lost. Of the poems, however, we are left with several quotations also in other works by Cicero himself. These fragments demonstrate the influence of one of the most important Latin poets, Catullus, and other neoterics.

Alphabetical overview of Cicero's poetic and epic-historical works

- *Alcyones*: epilogue composed by Cicero after 92 BC in which the myth of Alcyone and her husband Ceices was sung. Since these compared themselves to Jupiter and Juno in their wealth, pageantry and power, the gods made them shipwrecked during a sea voyage. Since Ceice died in the storm, Alcyone allowed herself to drown out of grief, so Jupiter turned both deceased into winged birds.

- *Aratea*: free juvenile translation of the *Heavenly Phenomena* by the Hellenistic poet Aratus of Soli.

- *De consulatu suo*: autobiographical poem composed by Cicero between 60 BC and 55 BC in which the author's rise to consulship and his victory in the trial against Lucius Sergius Catiline are discussed.

- *De temporibus suis*: another lost autobiographical work written in 54 BC in which Cicero celebrated his best actions during his consulship.

- *Epigrammata* ("Epigrams"): satirical compositions written by Cicero when he was in his early twenties. According to the accounts of the writer Quintilianus, the work was comic and ironic in genre and dealt with various fantastic and real topics.

- *Līmōn*: the title derives from the Greek noun Λειμών, "meadow"; this underscored the varied character of the work, a poem in hexameters in which a variety of literal and social topics were treated. Indeed, an account by Suetonius reports a harsh judgment of the author regarding a work by the playwright Terence.

- *Marius*: epic-historical poem in which Cicero discusses the exploits of consul Gaius Marius. The work is important for the author's transition from the Alexandrian genre to the historical genre mixed with poetry, that is, epic.

- *Nilus*: almost unknown work. Cicero is thought to have written it in praise of the qualities of Egypt's Nile River.

- *Pontius Glaucus*: an Alexandrian-style composition by Cicero. Written about 93 BC, the work dealt with the myth of Glaucus, who, after eating an aphrodisiac herb with magical powers, was transformed into a sea animal.

- *Tymhaeus*: extensive fragments of completed work on Plato's *Timaeus*, which Cicero presumably never published, merely preparing drafts of translations.

- *Uxorius*: work known almost exclusively through its title; it stands for *The Docile Husband* and therefore is believed to have had a joking character and light-hearted, if not overtly comic subject matter.

Epistolary

Cicero's epistles were rediscovered between 1345 and 1389 by Petrarch and the chancellor and humanist Coluccio Salutati. A total of about 864 letters were rediscovered, of which about ninety were written by correspondents, and this initially provoked great enthusiasm, tempered later by the fact that the image that transpired of Cicero was not that of the stalwart hero defender of the Republic, as he had always portrayed himself in his works and orations, but a much more human version, with its weaknesses and less rhetorical aspects, but certainly fascinating in their genuineness.

The epistles were collected and archived by Cicero's secretary Tyrone between 48 and 43 BC. They are divided into four categories:

- Epistles to Friends (*Epistulae ad familiares*) (16 books)

- Epistles to Brother Quintus (*Epistulae ad Quintum fratrem*) (3 books)

- Epistles to Marcus Junius Brutus () (2 books)

- Epistles to *Atticus (Epistulae ad Atticum*) (16 books)

II

MARCVS TVLL·CIC·FLOR·OLYM·174·
Ora vides Marcj Ciceronis, falsa sed illa:
Verior in libris extat imago meis.

Memory

Present throughout the Middle Ages, Cicero's memory flourished during the Renaissance; John I of Brandenburg prince-elector of Brandenburg in the 15th century was remembered after his death with the appellation *Cicero*, precisely because of his eloquence.

There are as many as four cities in the United States of America that have been given the name "Cicero" in honor of Marcus Tullius Cicero. In addition, the Latin expression *Cicero pro domo sua* is used to describe one who speaks advocating his own gain, but who more or less well masks the purpose of his speech as advocacy for another cause. It is derived from an oration delivered by Marcus Tullius in 57 B.C. to obtain the return of his own house, requisitioned from him during his exile.

Cicero's name has become antonomasia to refer to the guide who accompanies tourists on their visits to monuments and places, illustrating to them what they are visiting. Similarly, with the name Cicero are identified the revenue stamps, of different value (and color), but all bearing the effigy of the bust of Marcus Tullius Cicero, to be affixed to court documents, the proceeds of which feed the Lawyers' Welfare Fund.

Other books by United Library

https://campsite.bio/unitedlibrary

Milton Keynes UK
Ingram Content Group UK Ltd.
UKHW021435210923
429112UK00014B/728